# PURPOSELY
# CHOSEN

A MEMOIR

# PURPOSELY
# CHOSEN
## A MEMOIR

ANGELEE L. ALSTON

No Limit Publishers, LLC

Scripture quotations marked (KJV) are taken from the King James Version, public domain.

Scripture quotations marked (TLB) are taken from The Living Bible Version, copyright © 1971. Used by permission of Tyndale House Publishers, LLC Inc., Carol Stream, Illinois 60188. All rights reserved.

Scripture quotations (NLT) are taken from the *Holy Bible*, New Living Translation, copyright © 1886, 2004, 2015 by Tyndale House Foundation. Used by permission of Tyndale House Publishers, LLC Inc., Carol Stream, Illinois 60188. All rights reserved.

Scripture quotations (TM) are taken from The Message: The Bible in Contemporary English, copyright © 1993, 1994, 1995, 1996, 2000, 2001, 2002. Used by permission of NavPress Publishing Group. All rights reserved.

Printed in the United States of America
First Printing, 2019
ISBN 978-1-7333296-0-6
Published by:
No Limit Publishers, LLC
nolimitpublishersllc@gmail.com
www.NoLimitPublishers.com

Cover Design: DzineBK
Photography: Jackie Hicks
MUA:Letitia Thornhill
Editor:Jennifer Westbrook
Interior Design: Wendi Hayman

This is a work of creative nonfiction. The events are of the author's life and experiences. While all the stories in this book are true, some references and identifying details used were to recreate events, locales, and conversations from memories of them and are in no way meant to defame any person or place.

Ms. Taylor,

Thank you for your support. May God Bless you in all you do!

Angela Smith

# Dedication

*This book is dedicated to the chosen woman, my mother, who gave me life. Her life experiences showed me that true forgiveness may hurt beyond measure but is necessary in order to live on purpose. God created me through you, so I am part of you! Even though you didn't know how to conquer your addiction and illness to protect, guide and love me as your daughter, I still love you as my birth mother. I pray God will renew your mind and restore the lost years.*

*This is also dedicated to every woman and man who looks in the mirror and only sees that broken little girl or boy. To the one who stands alone and thinks no one will ever understand you, you are enough. To the one who is crazy enough to conquer their fears with boldness, you are Purposely Chosen!*

# Contents

# Acknowledgments

I would like to say a special thank you:

To my three sons, only God knows my heart for you. You are my reasons why I never give up. I promise, mommy will make you proud! I will stand strong with confidence, boldness, and dignity to fight for our purpose. You will be honored to be my sons. Thank you for your support and loving me despite what others thought or said of your mother. Continue to walk in your purpose my loves.

To my grandchildren, you are covered by God's Grace! Glam ma loves you!

To my "Nanny," who instilled the word of God in me. Without you, I never would have known to keep looking for God every time I messed up. I miss you so much, but grateful for the given years God allowed you in my life. Rest in Heaven my love, and I will make you proud to be your granddaughter.

To my birth mother, God gave me to you, to be your voice. My heart aches for your healing in every area of your life. Your pain will not be in vain. I love you!

To my birth father, God bless your soul.

To my brother, may God find you with an open heart.

To all my mother figures, especially those who have gone on to glory, thank you for being part of my life when I needed you. I will forever hold your words, hugs and corrective love dear to my heart.

To the amazing sisters from other mothers. Thank you for your encouragement, your advice, and your prayers. Thank you for pushing me when I needed it the most. Thank you for accepting me for who I am.

To my Mentors, God gave you gifts to help others following in your footsteps. Your passion and willingness to teach inspired me to grow and take to action! The accountability was challenging but worth it.

To my true love, you are the chosen one God has prepared just for me.

Forever grateful.

# Introduction

What can I say about myself? I am a uniquely designed woman who came to know and love God in a different way. I became a writer after being filled with so many emotions that I didn't know what to do, so I started writing for healing. When I was given an opportunity to share my story, I went for it. So here I am, an author and entrepreneur of many endeavors. I am a caring mother of three young men and grandmother of three wonderful grandchildren. My love and compassion for my children have encouraged me to never to give up on challenging experiences.

I am a survivor of countless occurrences of sexual, physical, and emotional abuse. I have endured these incidences as a child and unfortunately throughout adulthood. My life has changed tremendously in more ways than one. My determination to heal and stop generational curses has influenced my writing in private journals to release deep hurts that tried to control my personal relationships.

My passion for inspiring and educating others on childhood abuse has always been a desire within my reach. I know personally how childhood sexual abuse can have a wide range of effects on a child into their adulthood. It is my true goal to be an advocate for all children who have endured such abuse and trauma, which, in many instances, leads to mental illness. My vision is to have a facility that will honor and empower the strength of individuals to heal from any abuse.

My dedication to helping children motivated me to change my profession and pursue my passion for advocating for persons who need support in healing from traumatic experiences. I was so inspired that I created a support group called Restoration After Children's Emotions (R.A.C.E.).

R.A.C.E. will be a non-profit support organization that will help rebuild hope for children who have struggled with unimaginable difficulties. Their experiences may have affected their mental and emotional health and lead to irrational behaviors. R.A.C.E. will be a safe place to express concerns and will offer related recourses and counseling referrals for those who have had abusive or unwanted sexual experiences. R.A.C.E. will be a resource to break the cycle of generational curses within families.

My goals are to have more than enough funds to facilitate this vision through sponsorships and promoting my book, *Purposely Chosen*! This is just the beginning for so many men, women, and especially children to have a voice and live. God can restore what is broken and change it into something AMAZING!

# Chapter 1

# The Cost of the Oil in My Alabaster Box

One day, I was waiting for my son to come out from baseball practice. I was searching through the radio station when I hear the sweet songstress, CeCe Winans. "Yes! I love this song. God, help me hold back the tears!" I can't let these kids see me fall apart. Shake it off. Get yourself together now! I can do this! O.K. I am going to say this affirmation every day until something happens. "Today is the day I won't allow anything to take me off my course. Today, I will be happy! Today, I am going to show my kids how to be strong!

I often cried occasionally in front of them after holding in feelings for so long; it just came out, uncontrollable. I was trying to change the way I handled my hurts. Well that's what I told myself, "Today I am focusing on this". So, I am just going to close my eyes and recite these words in my head as I listen to this song. I can do all things through Christ Jesus who strengthens me!

*"The room grew still*

*As she made her way to Jesus*

*She stumbled through the tears*

*That make her blind*

*She felt such pain*

*Some spoke in anger*

*Heard folks whisper*

*There's no place here for her kind*

*Still on she came, through the shame that flushed her
face*

*Until at last, she spoke no words*

*Everything she said was heard*

*As she poured her love for the master*

*From her box of alabaster."*

I did it! I held it together. Ok, I still had tears; only it's happy ones this time. This song just does it to me every time. It used to bring up old memories of my dark places where somehow God rescued me. Have you ever had a song that just made you feel a certain way, whether sad or happy? Just like that, it touched your heart and soul, where you just wanted to react to it every time you heard it? Well, this song was a reminder of me pleading with God to help restore my inner being in every way that I was broken. I mean, I had heard of the different sayings and meanings of the song, but I needed to know exactly what those words "alabaster box" meant. Why did certain words stir up something in me? I had to research it more and look a little deeper into the history of Mary's alabaster's box cited in the Bible.

After reading several versions, this is what I got out of it. In the Bible days of Jesus, when a young woman reached the age of availability for marriage, her family would purchase an alabaster box for her and fill it with precious ointment. The size of the box and the value of the ointment would parallel her family's wealth. This alabaster box would be part of her dowry. When the young man came to ask for her hand in marriage, she would respond by taking the alabaster box and breaking it at his feet. The gesture of anointing his feet showed him honor.

After inquiring on this subject, I guessed its significance meant the value of precious oil intended for the man the young lady would marry one day. Funny, I didn't know anything about the importance of my oil because of all the traumatic abuse I had suffered. My oil was losing value with every experience. God was always there to give me hope; I just didn't know it for myself. Now, He has given me the grace to embrace the memories that were once hidden so deep inside that I forgot who I was as an individual. I didn't know my identity or even my self-worth. I was just existing; going with the flow in life. Everything I thought I wanted in life was not the assigned plan. Well, maybe part of it but it wasn't my destiny, which perfectly explains why some people were just seasonal.

"Where have you been for the last 40 years of my life, God? Have you really been with me like it says in your good book called the Bible? Did you really intend to make such a creation as me? Did you mean for me to endure such pain from sexual abuse, domestic violence, and mental abuse?"

I can't imagine you "love" me that much. I can't imagine you seeing me suffer through these things and saying you care for my wellbeing. Again, why God have you forsaken me?

Jeremiah 29:11 reads, "I know the plans I have for you, declares the Lord, plans to prosper you and not harm you, plans to give you hope and a future."

"Yes, my daughter, you were purposely chosen for this assignment." This is the answer I would self-consciously get after reading this scripture. Although I have read it many times, it didn't register before.

I would often hear other inspirational and motivational speakers on television and radio talk about certain issues that I could relate to. Pastors from churches would speak and quote the Bible on my concerns and situations I was going through. It seemed that God delivered and helped them overcome their test and trials which may have included some sort of abuse. I just didn't believe it for myself.

I never thought I would get an answer from God until now. God has really been with me during the whole time of my experiences. What was he thinking to choose me for this assignment? This has really been a challenge. At times, I didn't think I could last through all the disappointments from others. I started writing in my little pocket calendars years ago whenever I would have an emotional thought. I didn't think much of it by jotting down little notes on paper here and there about my feelings. I never even thought about journaling. It wasn't until I was faced with counselors for my own son that I learned how journaling was a good therapeutic tool for healing. It hit me; "I needed this as a child." I never heard of counsel for children back then. We were just seen and not heard.

My experiences have finally changed my life for the better. Everything that has occurred was all for my good, but it sure didn't feel that way years ago. I felt so alone. When was my time coming?

My mindset has changed now. My drive has changed, and my focus has changed. I am finally taking it all in and fighting for my life and my seed.

You've heard of folks saying never question God's purposes. Why not? Why isn't life fair? I needed to know the answer to "why" for so many of my questions. Until now, I didn't understand that there was always a plan for the "oil in my alabaster box." I was just existing, but there was a plan.

Where do I start? Why did I wait so long to say enough is enough? This isn't just for my son. I needed this help too. There was some unfinished business with my heart and soul that I tried to dismiss that needed healing. Now I am at this point in my life, thinking I must make it right for me. My mind, body and soul must be restored in order to live. I must be the anchor to stop the generational curses within my family. I must carry out this assignment to make my spiritual father proud to have given me such a task. I will no longer be ashamed of the journey that was predestined for me. If God brought it to me, he will bring me out of it. God will restore what is broken and change it into something amazing; all I need is faith. He will give me back everything that was lost.

# Chapter 2

## My Mother Couldn't and My Father Wouldn't

Have you ever wished you were someone else? Have you ever just wondered how it would be to be part of someone else's family? I used to wonder these things when I was a child. Sometimes it was just wondering if my mother and father were just like the families I saw on television. We all know those families were make-believe, but why couldn't my immediate family be like them? I wanted a sister to play with and tell her my secrets. I wanted lots of brothers to protect me and beat up bullies when I needed them. Wishful thinking got me nowhere. Although I grew up in a two-parent household in my early years, it wasn't the best for me. What I can remember is that my father worked all the time, and when he came home, he had his beers and slept. My mother worked outside the home as well. I remember her going out and having a good time with her friends occasionally. Being with her friends seemed more important than being my mother because I barely remember seeing her around for any of my important moments.

Looking back, I was born a preemie barely weighing 3 pounds, on November 27th, 1970. My father was going to be a father for the first time, and my mother was having her second live baby. She miscarried before having me. I never knew about this until I had a recent conversation with my mother about some experiences she had in her past. She told me I needed much more care and I was transported in an incubator. My precious life was in God's hands! Three months later, I was able to go home with my parents. I survived!

I vaguely remember any exciting childhood memories. Why is that? All children should have happy moments to remember, like stories of baking cookies and brownies. Did I block all my memories out to escape all that happened? It seemed like the bad overpowered any good in my life at the time. I remember my mother being a minister in the church. She would sing in the church choir and often preach a sermon. Sometimes she would do a holy dance and I would get so embarrassed. Why did she have to do all that? But in the back of the church, we all did a holy dance. I guess we caught the Holy Spirit, too. I also remember her in and out of the church. I started to think it was the norm for her to preach, sing, and shout on Sunday and go drink and get high later. I would hear her speaking something different when she said the prayer. Some called it "speaking in tongues." Something was strange about my mother's behavior. At home, she would do weird things in the house. She would sprinkle what appeared to be salt all over the house. She said it was to get rid of bad spirits.

I saw my mother in and out of the mental hospital. The hospital was right across from the main hospital where my father worked. How ironic for him to have to go see his wife right across from where he worked. When my brother and I got out of school, we would go visit her. I was scared to go into that place. Everyone acted weird to me, as if they were in slow motion. I felt angry at my mother for not being home, but sad to see her in a place like that. "Why are you here?" "I want you to come home with us." She would just look at me with concern but wouldn't speak like she truly cared. As a matter of fact, this was the norm for her. If I can remember, she was always in this state of mind. When she would come home, she was off to church. When she felt better, she was off to the same friends in the streets again. In the meantime, my brother and I were neglected and deprived of her motherly love and affection.

I remember one day my mother said, "Let's go riding little lady." I believe I was around six years old when she took me to one of her girlfriend's homes. We rode for a while into what seemed to be another town. I thought I was going to have so much fun, especially spending time with my mother. Her so-called, great friend came out to greet us and said, "Hi sweetie." We ended up going to a store to buy some snacks: pizza, soda pop, candy bars, and popcorn. All my favorites! What kid wouldn't like all this? It was major junk food. Once we got back to her friend's home, I was led to a back room. I can remember the television was so big that it sat on the floor with a large antenna on top of it.

As I was watching television and eating my favorites, I heard loud music and other voices. I was ok until I started smelling an aroma that had a weird smell. I now know it was weed. It wasn't funny anymore. I yelled for my mommy. She never came to the door. I tried turning the knob; it was locked. Where was she? It seemed like hours had gone by. I cried myself to sleep. I was awakened by the creaking of the door opening. It was my mommy! I was just happy to see her. It was the next day, I think, because it was evening when we arrived, and now it was daylight. She gazed at me and said, "Let's go!" She didn't even notice my clothes were wet when we got in the car to go home. I never said a word. I thought I could depend on her. She was supposed to be my mommy who protected me, or was she? Why was she sometimes there with us and sometimes not? Where was she going at night? Why was it lonely at night when I went to bed? Where was my brother? When was my dad coming home? I had all these questions in my head about everyone.

If I can remember, my dad worked in the evening. He would leave while we were at school and returned around midnight. A little girl's memories of her dad should be nothing but the best of the best, so why do I only have memories of destruction in my head? My father would come home at night from work and come into the room and stand over me. I would pretend to be sleeping, hoping he would go away. He would stand there so long that I would eventually fall asleep. I would wake up hours later with my not yet fully developed breast exposed. I would think to myself, "this has to be a dream."

Other times, he would go farther with his selfish acts of indecency with me. He would fondle my breast from side to side. I would pray to God, asking for my mom to come in the room. Where was she at? I was still pretending to be sleep. I felt so weird about all this coming from him. I never knew when it would stop. I started to develop an inner person to block my feelings about what was happening to me outside my body. My inner person didn't feel anything. She spoke to me with calmness. She was so strong. She never left my side. She was there to protect me. My angel! Close your eyes and it will be ok. Are you seeing this God? Where are you?

Another memory I have is when I was around ten years old, but all I know is that my mom was not in the home with me. I don't remember if she was just out or institutionalized. I had the worst pain in the lower part of my stomach. I had to go to the bathroom bad. I pulled the covers back on my bed and saw traces of blood. What's going on here? I was terrified. I ran out from out my bedroom to go to the restroom and there he was, walking around naked and standing with the refrigerator door open, with a hard-on. Do I tell him what just happened? I was frozen in my tracks. Was this a dream? Or was it a reality? Was this normal to do while your children were there in the house? I later realized it was my period. Since I learned in health class what this was and heard all the girls talking about it, I knew what I needed from the bathroom. Luckily, my mother had sanitary items under the bathroom sink. How embarrassing. For some reason, I don't remember my brother being around.

I must have blocked so many episodes of things that happened to me because they never seemed real. They didn't start to surface until after I was grown up and married and had children of my own. Although I would have nightmares, I would try to dismiss them. These memories were still there in the back of my head, even when I tried to make amends with my father on different occasions. I never understood why I didn't have that "Father and Daughter Love." My mother was absent so much from my life due to her addictions and mental state of mind. He ended up having to take on the responsibility of raising two kids when she couldn't do it. I am grateful that my Nanny stepped in as much as she could to help. My time was back and forth with her. Her niece stepped in to care for me when she went to work. Going back home with my dad was confusing. I felt unsafe, but why? I thought I was the "apple" of his eye. What did I do to deserve any of this from him?

One Christmas holiday was one of the saddest days ever in my childhood. My mom wasn't there. What kept her from coming home on Christmas Eve and Christmas Day? I had to keep dealing with my father. He kept coming in my room for his pleasure. I honestly don't remember how many times this happened. It was a nightmare that wouldn't go away! I felt hopeless! I would cry out, "Please help me, God." "Please help me, mommy."

"Please help, Nanny." No one was there.

My mother couldn't love me like I wanted her to love me. She wouldn't hold me in her arms and tell I could be anything I wanted to be. I needed her to talk to me about what life was about to bring me. I needed her to show me how to handle disappointments as a woman. I needed her to talk to me about womanhood.

My father wouldn't love me the way he was supposed to. I needed protection from all the bad things that came my way unexpectedly. I needed him to tell me I was beautiful and treat me like his princess. I wanted all the things little girls dreamed of. I never had a birthday party with all the pretty decorations. Just to be a princess for a day would have been wonderful.

In the summer of 1984, I went to live with my Nanny for a great length of time. I felt so safe with her. She was always trying to fatten me up. I was always a tiny little girl for my age. I loved to eat her cooking but never seem to gain. She was great at down-home-cooked meals. The buttermilk biscuits just melted in your mouth, and then was topped with Grandma molasses. She knew she had to be mindful of what she ate because of her diabetes. It never stopped her from cooking though.

I loved going to church with her to see her sing in the choir. I could count on her to take me with her to church. I felt good there but always wondered why we were not getting our prayers answered. I kept my thoughts to myself. I was ashamed of what she would think of me.

When my parents finally got a divorce, I didn't know how to handle it. I mean, I was happy, but what did that mean for me? My mother wasn't around anyway because she was doing her thing in the streets. I didn't care to stay with my father, either. He was already with another woman and her child. I loved them both, but they didn't show the right love to me. Instead of going back and forth between them and my Nanny, I wanted to stay with her. I begged to stay with my Nanny. It was best to stay with Nanny. Who knew I would still have to face my fears while living with her?

# Chapter 3

## Unwanted Love

I was really enjoying myself living with my Nanny. Since my parents were unsettled about me during the divorce, I stayed with Nanny for the following year for middle school. I didn't talk much at first, but soon I started hanging with some girls from the neighborhood. Everyone that I came across wasn't so nice. Some girls teased me. For what? I didn't know them. They made fun of everything. My clothes, my size, my hair. I tried fixing my hair all the time because I was trying to make it look like my mother took me to the hair salon. I wanted my hair to look nice like the other girls. I wanted the fancy clothes and shoes. This is probably where my interest in doing hair came from. I always loved putting my hair in different styles. Overall, I focused on my schoolwork and made good grades. I was going to make everyone proud of me. I wanted this so badly so I could get away from everyone—except for my Nanny.

I used to walk the neighborhood with the other girls, cutting through certain paths between homes. Along the way, I used to pick up a couple of little plums that fell on the ground. The trees were so full of plums that they would be everywhere, overflowing from the private yards. We all knew better than to go into anyone's yard to try to get any fruit. I remember making myself sick from eating so many plums. I loved pouring salt on them. I ate so many that my tongue was extremely sore. Not to mention, it was the most powerful laxative ever!

There were these neighborhood boys who used to ride their bikes all around the neighborhood. One day, I had just left one of the girls' homes and started to go back to my Nanny's house. I had gone through this path many times and never had an encounter with anyone. This day was different. I could hear the sounds of immature comments from the boys behind me. They were riding small dirt bikes and following me as I attempted to move from side to side to get out their way. At first, I thought to myself that they were just horsing around and would keep it moving. But no, one stopped his bike in front of me. I recognized his face because he used to come around to play with my cousin. The others I didn't really know, but I knew they were from the neighborhood. They were also much older than me. Suddenly, I found myself on the ground with what seemed like spiders all over me. I was swinging at the spiders, only to realize it was their hands that were pulling on my shirt and shorts at the same time. I screamed at them as they giggled at my struggle to get away. It made me have a flashback.

I couldn't just lay there like I did with my father. Too many of them. What am I going to do? HELP ME GOD! You must come through for me. I was so scared. I started kicking and scratching with all my might when I heard a timid voice say, "Let her go." With my clothes almost uncovering me, I got up and ran all the way to my Nanny's house. Tears covered my eyes so heavily that I could barely see where I was going. I told her about what happened. She relayed everything to my mom, and they decided to take me to the police station. At least they agreed on something. Wow, finally someone believes me.

It was a scary process. Once their names came up in the system, we found out this was not their first time being in this type of trouble with approaching girls. Apparently, they had struck out and had to go to court. I was summoned to testify about my experience to determine their consequences. My stomach had knots in it when I walked into the courtroom. The parents' sneers made me even more reluctant to say anything. I had to go sit up front with the judge. "What's going on here!?" This man is yelling at me. He said I was lying about what happened. Did they trick me into coming here? Why was everyone looking at me like I did something wrong? I was humiliated for telling the truth. I cried on the stand and looked for my mother to comfort me. Did she believe me?

When I went back to school, it was as if everyone knew about it. Rumors started to spread like a wildfire.

Did this make the paper? Well, I thought it did. Those boys were in hot water and had some charges brought against them. They were cut from their high school basketball team. I believe one or two had to attend reformatory school because the other kids mentioned it. I could hear the remarks at the school, on the bus, and around the neighborhood. I couldn't concentrate anymore on my schoolwork. My grades started to drop. I didn't want to go to school anymore.

My life was affected by this. To this day, I feel anxiety over entering a courtroom. I didn't want to say anything about this to anyone ever again.

I was getting older, and my body was changing into something I didn't understand. I hurt so bad when I had my monthly flow. I knew I didn't like any part of becoming a woman. I would hurt so bad that it made me want to crawl under a bed and stay there until it went away. I didn't want to worry my Nanny, so I didn't talk to her about how I felt about anything, even though I trusted her.

I would be around certain family members and wouldn't talk as much. The trauma wouldn't allow me to express myself to anyone. Maybe I had so much in me to tell but didn't know how to trust anyone to talk to.

I remember another family member who took advantage of their sick desires. This one family member was always touching me inappropriately when no one was watching. When they would become intoxicated with alcohol and high with anything else, it would start. He would catch me every time I was alone and fondle me erotically with his fingers and mouth. I started to feel like I was just a target for this kind of abuse. Tears would just stream down my face. When he would finish, he just laughed at me. I thought to myself, "What was so darn funny?" I was sick to my stomach every time I would see him during family events. I didn't want to say anything to anyone. No one would have believed me anyway.

Now I had these sexual tendencies that I couldn't explain. I was so confused.

Where was my mother? Where was God? I pretty much had to fend for myself. I was determined that I was going to finish school and do something with my life. Despite what I had been through, I had dreams of going places I had never seen and doing something big in my life. Yes, that would show everyone that did something to me that I was going to make it.

My mom and I tried making amends. I went back to live with her in another town away from my Nanny. She gave my Nanny so much grief about things I was getting into. Figure that. What was going to be different with her? I was facing high school now. I really needed her. Maybe she was going to change to get me through high school. She of course, was back to being herself. She cursed me out every chance she had. Why was I there? Oh yeah, it was a money thing. She never wanted me there with her. It was about the child support that I never saw. She didn't want my Nanny to get anything out of it. In a way, I didn't care about anything from my father. I just wanted my mother to be my mother.

I remember her slapping me in front of one of my cousins just because I asked for lunch money. I grew angry with her every time she said or did anything to me. She had no clue where she was taking me. Anyway, there we were again. She was never there for me. My brother and I literally had an apartment to ourselves. Basically, I was sending myself to school because he was hardly ever there. We were eating whatever was there in the house to eat. We had too much freedom as a teenager with no guidance. This was not that love we wanted or needed.

# Chapter 4

## Nanny

My dear Nanny, that's what I called her. I would love it when she would hug me so tight. She would smell like Oil of Olay moisturizer. I felt so safe, loved and spoiled when I was with her. I just wanted to stay right there in her bosom. She was my rock to get through my little crying spells. My brother and I would go stay with her during some summers and holidays. I was such a crybaby at times.

"Girl, hush that fuss up," is what my Nanny would say. She had no idea or understood why I cried in her presence? I needed her to know I was craving my parents' love, but I didn't know how to explain it to her.

Nanny's health was a challenge for her, which caused her to travel to multiple doctors out of town. Since she lived long distance from the doctors' offices, she would stop by our home before traveling back to her home. Unfortunately, she would come through when my brother and I were left alone. She would steam with anger when she saw we were there with no food. "Where is your mother at? Go get in the car right now!" I was scared because I knew what would happen if my mother came home and found my brother and I gone. It was going to cause a war between these two. I would hear the arguments they would have when my grandma would chastise my mother about our care. My mother had something against my grandmother. What was it that caused such hostility between them? I knew they love each other but sometimes it was hard to tell.

Long as I can remember, my Nanny could put down a piece of cooking. Ahhh, just aroma from the kitchen was like walking into a restaurant to me. The menu she prepared seem like Thanksgiving every day. The memory of her standing in the kitchen with a worn red waist apron, often comes to me when I am standing in the kitchen. It was the aroma of homemade buttermilk biscuits and Grandma's molasses, that kept me in the kitchen with her. She would occasionally catch me peeping from the side door of the opening into the kitchen and tell me, "Come on in here girl and learn something." The lessons started in the kitchen with her, but she never once spoke of her own worries to me. She didn't have a clue that I knew of her concerns. I saw it on her face. I was the child that was seen and not heard.

Although my Nanny was a church going woman, she worried about her husband. He would hang out at the "trailer liquor store" all night. She would worry about her son's bisexual behavior. She would most definitely worry about my mother, who had issues of alcohol, drugs and patterns of mental illness. She never gave up on praying for them, as I could see. I saw her go to church, sing in the choir, and participate in functions. What I didn't get was why her praying didn't change them. I could feel her hurt. Where are you, God? Make her hurt go away.

Nanny didn't deserve certain things that were happening to her. I only saw the good in her. She was my "She-ro." When I asked her about why she was suffering from medical issues, she would reply, "Oh, I haven't been saved by God all my life; as long as God gives me grace, I will be fine."

Long as I could remember, my Nanny loved her husband. Although he wasn't my real grand-father I loved him just the same. I never had a chance to meet my mother's father. My step-grandfather was funny. I remember the times he would come in late smelling like a liquor barrel. All you could hear was my Nanny's voice yelling at him. She was highly upset with him for spending unnecessary money. He would just say "I got it," in a low tone.

The one thing that stood out to me, was what he told my grandmother right before he passed. He told her, "Angie is pregnant." "OMG" How did he know that? I never told him anything. I guess it's true what they say this cliché, "when one family member dies out the family, there's one born into the family."

I didn't think Nanny would ever marry again after her first husband passed. I didn't like Nanny's second husband. He was a mean snake behind closed doors. She met him in church—well figure that. When I found out he was verbally abusive to her, I wanted to lay hands on him. She never wanted anyone to know about the abuse or say anything to him if they did know. Maybe she was just embarrassed because of church folks. I would hear her say, "God is going to take care of it." I vowed never to get married because I hadn't seen any good marriages so far. Where are you God? Make her hurt go away. She doesn't deserve this from anyone.

Despite what she went through, Nanny found time to pray and read the Bible to me. Sometimes I understood, and sometimes I didn't. I can truly say it's because of her that I knew something about God's forgiveness. She lived it. She always told me, "One day you're going to be the one to take care of your mother. God gave you to her for a reason. Stay in the church and God will see you through."

In my early years I would dress in baggy clothes like a little boy. I wore oversized t-shirts and jeans. My hair was to my shoulders, so I wore it pulled back in a pony-tail. Nanny would tell me to start dressing like a girl. I didn't feel pretty like a girl. I wanted to hide everything that made me look like a girl. I never told her of my nightmares. I wondered why she loved God so much. He didn't seem to be helping either one of us.

I miss my Nanny now. I remember, while I was with my family across the waters overseas, she closed her eyes to go home to glory. I remember clear to this day when she asked me if I would be back to go to her funeral. Why would she say something like that? Did she know she wasn't going to be here long?

I need her to be here now, to converse and give me advice. I need her here, so I can get a motherly hug from her. She gave the best mother hugs. I need to smell her scent of Oil of Olay-moisturized skin. I just need her to call me and say one more time, "It's going be ok. Just trust God. He will see you through." I remember her slapping her hand down on her knee before singing, "I know the Lord will make a way."

One suggestion she made to me was to start a career for myself. She told me to not depend on a man for all your needs. She said, "Always have your own nest egg for you and your children." To this day, I wish I had made that decision back then for myself like she told me. I wanted to be loved by a man so much that I jumped at the chance to be a wife and follow my high-school sweetheart in his career. I didn't see it in myself to go for my own dreams. Nanny always told me, "If you marry, you must be submissive to him. You can't go do things on your own. Honor and respect this man as your husband. God will bless you for being his wife." Maybe that's one of the reasons I stayed in certain situations. Even though I was told these things from her, I didn't see it for my-self to be so submissive. She wouldn't tell me anything wrong, so I tried my best to do just that.

Well, she did it. My Nanny married her second hus-band. I didn't care for him that much. It was something about him that I didn't like but if he was going to make her happy, then I was ok with it. Long and behold, this guy was an old trickster. My Nanny carried herself with class, and she took care of whatever she had. I believed she was smitten by his attention for her. He of course, liked what he saw and wooed her to fall for his intentional schemes. What did she see in him? Was she longing for companionship so bad that she settled? He spoke to her with any kind of way with verbal abuse. I heard he also physically abused her. She didn't take smack off her first husband, so I know she wouldn't be taking it off her second husband. Some cousins of mine were going to find him and do a little talking to him, if you know what I mean. I became angry once I heard of such things he said and did to her. Thankfully, she got out of the situation with him. It was then that I saw marriage as a bad thing after seeing my mother and grandmother's failed marriages.

The signs of this vicious cycle were hard to ignore; within my family, I saw one marriage fall apart after another. Only I had no clue that I was following in their footsteps! My Nanny nor my mother had a clue of our generational curse.

# Chapter 5
## Why Am I Here?

I never understood my mother and father's rejection of me. All I wanted from them was their parental love and guidance for me to grow into adulthood. What were their goals for me? Why did they have any children if they were not ready to be parents? Why was I born to them as their child? My mother and I never seemed to see eye to eye once I became a teenager. She didn't even get along with my Nanny. Their relationship seemed just as awkward as me and my mother's relationship. I often wondered why it was like that. All I saw was resentment from my mother towards Nanny.

I asked my Nanny, "Why does she hate me so much?" Is it because I looked like my father so much that she couldn't love me the way she should have? So many people said that I looked like my father. I think it made her mad to hear that all the time. She would be mean to me at times when she would get a little tipsy after having a drink or two. I remembered her favorite drink came with a little purple bag with gold trim and a drawstring. It had a name printed on it called "Crown Royal." I think it was her best friend because it was always around when everything was confusing for her.

She was supposed to be "mom," but she didn't sound like a mother to me. I remember those days when she was not herself. "Get out of my way you little hoe…. Sit your ugly a$$ down before I slap the hell out of you…. Don't ask me for no money, little a$$hole." That comment came with a slap after I questioned her one time about money being sent from my father for child support payments. I hated to call him for anything so I would ask my Nanny for what I needed. She would then argue over who would give me lunch money or any other school supplies I needed.

I used to think to myself, how could you call me those names when I've seen you with different men, doing things that were wrong. Most of all, you were never there for me when I needed you to be. I needed you during elementary school during school plays. During middle school, you weren't there. You never even showed up to pick me up after a sports tryout.

During the most memorable moments of high school, my mother wasn't there. I would go to bed and wake up without her there and would go to school every day, not knowing where she was. I hungered for her to hold me and talk to me as her daughter even as a teenager. I started to yearn for love from whoever and wherever I could get it. Why am I here God?

One evening, my mother was a different person, and I feared what was going to happen. She must had been high or drunk because she wanted to fight me over money I didn't have. I had to call the police because she wouldn't allow me to leave her house. Since, I was underage, I had to stay and tuff it out with her. I had to be 18 in order to move out. That's what the police told me.

This wasn't the only time she became violent. She was so upset about something and I was the one around for the cursing and fussing, only this time it came with a backhand across the face. Never saw it coming. It left marks, especially because she had rings on her fingers. Was it my fault that she and my dad got a divorce? Was it my fault she didn't want me around? Was it my fault my father behaved in a sexual way towards me? What was the meaning of all this? God, why would you allow these things to happen to me? I truly didn't understand any of this. I was depressed and didn't realize what I was going through. I wanted a way out.

I continued to wonder if there was a God—the one my mother prayed to off and on. The one she talked about in the pulpit when she decided that church was for her. The one my father sang songs about, standing up at the front during praise and worship. Those two didn't look like God was in them to me. I saw and felt different from them. Sometimes I wished to be in another family. I felt alone and didn't want them as my parents anymore.

Nanny prayed to the same God. She kept praying no matter what she went through. If she was having a bad day, even when she was sick, she didn't complain. At least I never knew of any complaints. I even asked her, "Why do you suffer when you serve God?" She would answer that she didn't always serve God, and she asked God for grace and mercy every day. What was she trying to say to me? That God would allow such things to happen in your life but would give you the strength to get through it?

My Nanny's words to me were to "Treat them with respect and honor them. One day you may be the one to take care of them, and they will see what a great gift you are to them." I began to have hatred in my heart for them both. I needed a way out but didn't know which way to go. I didn't understand those words from her until now.

Psalm 27:10 (The Living Bible) says, "For if my father and my mother should abandon me, you would welcome and comfort me."

Psalm 27:14 (The Living Bible) says, "Don't be impatient. Wait for the Lord, and he will come and save you! Be brave, stouthearted, and courageous. Yes, wait and he will help you."

# Chapter 6

# The Beginning of My Soul Ties

The definition of a soul tie is this: A spiritual connection between two people who have been physically intimate with each other or who have had an intense emotional or spiritual association or relationship that ties one person's life to another. I had no idea what it meant to have a soul tie with someone. I started to hear about this in church and began to research its meaning. I even purchased books that spoke about it. "When you have sex with someone, married or not, there's a spiritual bond created. The soul-tie is so powerful that even when you are no longer with that person, they are still with you in memories, scents, music, and places." (*Soul-Ties,* by RC Blakes, Jr.) It was relatable to what I had been enduring in my relationships with men. What if the intimacy was with someone that was making unwanted advances? How does that work from unwanted physical or emotionally association? I wondered how this definition applied to my physical, emotional, and spiritual state throughout the years.

My first child was born when I was 18 years old. My need for male bonding lead to this soul tie; I was infatuated with someone that I grew up with. Our mothers knew each other, so I spent quite a lot of time around his family. I was curious, and he showed me some attention. I was already exposed to touches that made me feel like that was just who I was to everyone. This feeling was different though; it felt ok to be with him—or so I thought. I wasn't scared to be with him. I didn't cringe at his touch. I wanted him to do whatever to show his attraction to me. It was my first "puppy love." I didn't care if it was wrong or not. Besides, no one was there to tell me any different. These feelings started me falling for someone that I thought felt the same way. Boy, was I wrong! I was a joke to him. I heard him laugh to the other boys one day, about what I thought was our special moment. I even remembered the song that was playing "Where Do Broken Hearts Go" by Whitney Houston. How ironic.

He and his friends joked around about how I lost my virginity to him. I grew angry with him. How could he tell them anything about us? Probably, because it was no us. Just my luck, I became pregnant. I told him about the pregnancy, but he was not feeling it. He said the baby was not his and accuse me of being with others. Like any young man, he was scared and failed to show his true feelings by pushing me away. He didn't want to have anything to do with me. I was devastated that he didn't care. He couldn't see that I needed him to be there for the baby and me. What was wrong with me that I didn't matter?

Nine months later, I had a son. I loved him with all my heart. I was a scared teen mom who had no idea what I was about to get into as a young mother. I still had my final year in high school to finish. How was I going to do this with no help? I ended up dropping out and going to night school so I could finish. I had to leave my high school friends behind to be mommy.

I didn't know how to be a parent. There were no instructions when it came down to the early feedings and the crying for no reason. I only knew that I wanted to give him everything I didn't have—the right love. He was mine, all mine; a real baby doll. I had to protect him from anything that meant him any harm. Something was still missing for me. I still wanted his father to be part of us. Only one thing: he had a girlfriend. "Young and dumb" is what they call it. Just silly teenagers who had no clue about experimenting with adult roles.

When I found out she had a son too, I had a meltdown because he was there for her during her pregnancy. Well, I guess you can say this was the beginning of one of my rejections by someone I wanted to be with. I had a connection with him that left me numb inside, a soul tie. Because of my baby boy, I felt like nothing mattered as long as I had my baby. Seeing him brought me joy. So, why was I crying all the time? It seems some days, I cried all day. Some days, he cried all day. Other days we just cried together, looking at each other. I didn't know what to do for him. I thought I could handle being a mother on my own. Here's where the repercussions of having premarital sex as well as unprotected sex started. I had a little human being that tied me to my son's father no matter what. Even though we didn't stay connected physically, my emotional state was affected.

My mother gave me a really hard time after my baby boy came into the world. I worked at the food chain, Burger King, and saved enough money to get into my own place. I was able to apply for an apartment, and even though it was through the city's housing authority, it was all mine. I had no choice but to groom myself to be a mother. Motherly instinct kicked in to care for him. Who cares if the rest of them didn't want to be part of our lives? I was going to go back to school and make this work.

I would have thought I learned from the earlier part of my life to focus on myself and my baby boy. My Nanny told me to sign up for the military and go get a career for myself. She told me she would take care of my little one until I returned from basic training. What was I afraid of? I had my own agenda. I had my own way of thinking. Instead, I was still yearning for love from a male. It probably wouldn't matter who showed me love at the time because I was in a vulnerable state.

This next soul tie was someone I knew from the school I attended while living with my Nanny. He had this walk that I would always remember. It had a little "swag" to it. Whatever it was, I was attracted to it. Since he showed an interest in my son and me, I was on board with going out with him. We began having a relationship. We shared intimate conversations about our families. He was raised by a single mother and didn't have a close relationship with his father either. He was hurt and angry about his father spending more time with other ladies and their children. He had my heart already.

We spent so much time together that eventually we were together intimately. He shared his hurts about his father, and I could relate to him, but I couldn't bring myself to tell him everything about my father. I would just say, "I am not close to my father." He saw the struggle his mother went through with the fathers of her children. Although I knew about his anger and bitterness towards his certain concerns, I thought we could help each other. I thought he could understand my hurts in my past and love me for me, but I was still hesitating to talk about everything. I didn't take into consideration how we were going to be together if we both needed help with our own hurts. At the time, I didn't pay attention to the insecurities he had with his own mother and father and how it would affect my child and us as a couple or even having more children. I needed his attention, and I felt he needed mine. I didn't know any better, and I didn't realize that I was still on the road to self-destruction. I had no clue that because of this generational curse, I was heading down a path that was truly going to affect me the rest of my life.

Neither of us had an idea of what a real relationship looked like or felt like. We were playing house and had no clue as to what responsibilities or consequences came with living together.  We really thought we knew what we were doing.

We were pregnant with my second child and his first. Sound familiar? Just like my mother.  I was repeating the cycle all over again.  No matters to me once I saw my baby's face. This little fellow was the spitting image of his father. I was so excited for us, but we needed a plan. Although we loved each other, we were not mature enough mentally and were still heading for destruction. Babies are cute and adorable, but they can't solve deep issues. He was hot tempered, and I was resentful. What a combination. Rumors floated around about his involvement with other women. Family and friends tried telling me of his promiscuous ways. I didn't want to believe any of it. It was time to breakup!

I became vulnerable again. I was broken again. I was angry again. I was bitter again. I didn't care about how I was going to get love anymore, until……

Here I go heading down the road of loneliness.  I mean the trap to loneliness. Yes, that one co-worker understood what I was going through. He noticed that I didn't have money to buy lunch all the time. He would offer to buy me lunch. How could I say no when my stomach said yes? Conversations were easy with him. Since I didn't have a car, he offered rides to and from the job. Then came the offers to have lunch outside the job. Why not? What harm could it do? I found myself in a situation so fast.  He told me I was beautiful. He showered with gifts. After one night of lust and loneliness, he said I belonged to him. He started to be controlling on the job and made threats if I spoke to anyone of the opposite sex. It was a cost for all this attention I was getting from him. On one drive home he kept going, just driving right pass my drop off. He began to speak of his "real" job. He spoke of how the yellow "Caution" tape would be around my apartment; only no one would find me.

With one hand on the steering wheel and the other on the back of my neck squeezing tight, I began to pray in my head. It was obvious that he was using his day job as a decoy for his "distributing" career. Everything started making sense—the nice clothes, nice cars, and big roll of bills. He gave me money when I didn't even ask for it. I didn't pay attention to all that stuff because I just wasn't used to it. I was naïve to the street life. How was I going to get out of this car? All I could think about was my boys. Where are you God? Then, suddenly he stopped and told me to get out of his car. I walked home, crying all the way. It didn't even seem that far, but it was quite a distance. Once I got home, I held my boys and vowed to make it right for them. I didn't know what to do about the job but later found out that he quit. I never heard from him again. I never spoke of this to anyone. God gave me another chance to get it right.

My reconciliation with my second child's father wasn't hard to do at the time. We eventually got married. Yes, I married him. I wanted this to work so badly. Overall, I loved him. I wanted the idea of having a husband, the children, the dog, and the house with the white picket fence. I didn't see the toxicity of the relationship. I didn't like my situation but didn't know what to do about it. I didn't trust the warning signs of his flirtatious ways and the little lies. Neither one of us was mentally ready for marriage. I hadn't seen any lasting marriages in my family before, so why did I go through with it? He never knew what a successful marriage looked like either. So why was I willing to go into it, knowing what I knew? Like I said, I liked the idea of having a different life from my mother and having a successful marriage.  Plus, I didn't want to be alone with two children, no career, and no stability. I made a choice to follow him in every kind of way as his wife. This was my identity—mommy and wife.

Throughout the course of the marriage, there were still lies, cheating, and manipulation. I, on the other hand, had temptations from other men who showed me affection.

I trusted my husband to do the right thing by me and the boys. I settled because I didn't think I had a choice in the matter, and no one would want me with two children. He would flirt with other women right in my face, and I would overlook it. He said it was to get us things and it didn't mean anything. He knew I loved the church, and he would purposely do things to agitate me. He would ask me to do things that I knew wasn't right, but out of my submission to him, I complied.

He eventually attended and got involved in church. I was excited that things were turning around. This meant we had to work this out. God doesn't honor divorce, right?

We had mutual friends that came to me and told me

about his advances to certain women in our circle. I never wanted to believe that it was true, but then the boyfriends or husbands would say something about his intentions. These men made threats to him, and some were ready to do harm. Why was I ready to defend someone who didn't care how this affected the children or me? Had I been so manipulated that I didn't want to see the obvious right in front of me?

My most devastating moment with him was when he cheated with my stepsister, who was my father's stepdaughter. Of all the people in the world, why her? I felt she had the advantage of having my father as a real father to her, and now this. To make matters worse, it came from my father. How humiliating! I was crushed. I was confused. I was angry. After crying my tears into jugs, I wanted to get even with everyone. I went into a state of depression. No one understood the pain of betrayal I felt from all of them. I didn't trust anyone now. I was just learning to forgive and build some type of communication with my father. He failed me again. He didn't protect me. He had the nerve to say that my then-husband took advantage of my stepsister. I always wondered—even to this day—why she never pressed charges against him if that was true. I shouted at him; I hit him. I screamed at him. All he could say was, "She always wanted what you had." What did that mean? Was this another punishment from God? I was trying to fix it. How were we going to recover from this?

I needed my mother. I needed my Nanny. I needed God. "God, where are you again? God, are you real?

I can't take this anymore." I was in such a state that I couldn't even take care of the kids properly. I didn't function like a mother or anything for that matter. They were school age and knew something was not right.

I remember that my Nanny, mother, and a cousin showed up at my home afterward. They hadn't heard from me in a while. I was not communicating with them. I didn't want to hear anything they had to say. It was as if I was in the room but not in the room. I felt detached from my senses. I felt a detachment from everyone, even myself.

I didn't understand the Bible entirely. My Nanny would speak from her experiences and would include scriptures. She said, "God can get you through this. "I don't understand why you are going through this, but I know God is preparing you for something big." "He can even heal your marriage, if it's in the plan." "Trust that he will carry you through." I loved and respected my Nanny, but she didn't understand what I was going through. Maybe if I told her about my fears, she could've guided me on my choices in men. I wanted to leave everyone and never look back.

The opportunity presented itself for me to get out the marriage, but I didn't. I stayed with him. Certain family members talked about my choice to stay with him. I was ashamed of everything. The stronghold was real. It was a connection I couldn't let go. Again, I didn't know I had grounds to get out of the marriage. I was trying to stick it out. I gave it my all and decided to hold on no matter what.

In between the military travel to different duty stations, our marriage was spiraling down. The arguments were getting worse. They eventually became physical. I was an emotional wreck to the point that I didn't feel I had a choice in anything. He would speak to me in a manner like I was one of his soldiers. I remember my kids hearing a commotion after arriving home from school. My former husband had pushed me and slammed me down on the floor. As a result, I ended up with my arm in a sling and a sore body. He only received an order to attend an "Anger Management Class." After all that had happened, I still felt the need to cling to him. What did I have to go back to without him?

It is said that a Christian is supposed to forgive. I tried doing the right thing. I wasn't a wild girl in the streets. I went to church because I felt good there. The mothers of the church said to pray about it. God was supposed to heal my marriage—or was he? I followed my husband to wherever the military ordered him to go. I was a supportive and submissive wife. Why did I go through so many disappointments again?

Yeah, that part about being submissive.... I could hear those exact words ringing in my ears from Nanny. She said I had to be submissive to my husband as an honor. At this point, I was going through the motions of being a wife. Sometimes I wanted to be intimate with him, and sometimes I didn't. It was literary killing me inside. I wanted out, but I wanted my kids to have their father around and not be without him in the home. I didn't realize the harm it did to my children and myself by staying. My connection to my former husband wouldn't allow me just to turn him away sexually. See, I craved it, but I also despised it. Not only did I see him, but all my offenders were in my head in the moment of intimacy. It would play over and over like a video. Funny thing is, the video only came to me in my dreams or when I had an urge for a touch.

I became pregnant again. Only this time, it was an ectopic pregnancy. I lost my baby. I had a name for what I thought was my baby girl. This sent me into another depression. Was I being punished for my sins? I don't even know of my sins anymore. When I think I am doing right, I get disappointed all over again.

I needed this baby to make it right with him. Maybe he would have seen the baby and just fallen in love with us. Was this a sign for us to call it quits? I had no feelings. I felt numb. I felt pain in my heart but couldn't express it. I was going into a state of mind that was unexplainable.

In 2005, I was given a gift. It happened! It was a gift from God that was going to change everything. I welcomed my third son. I knew he had to be special because I stayed so sick and stressed out during my pregnancy. The baby finally arrived after two prior false labors. After reflecting on the one baby I lost before him, I knew then he was meant to be, despite what was going on around him. He was given to us for a reason. I had one more reason to make things right.

Even though he was born one month earlier than his due date, he was healthy. I still went through more stressful times within the marriage. I thought he would change after the baby arrived. He finally told me he didn't love me anymore. We argued over so many ridiculous things like moving into a house that we couldn't afford. Finances, children, our new baby, and the relationship in general caused a hardship on the whole family.

My boys were old enough to hear the verbal abuse and see the physical abuse. I knew how this would affect them but chose to stay even if it meant sacrificing my own happiness. In the long run, it did my boys more harm than good. They were angry and bitter toward both of us as their parents. I had lost my boys' respect as well. One of my sons even told me, "You allowed my dad to run all over you."

I made so many mistakes with choosing a male to love because of my issues with my mother and father. I didn't want my children to miss out on having a loving male role model in the home. I later realized that I had no clue then what a positive male role model was and why this was affecting us.

At the beginning of this chapter, I mentioned the beginning of my "soul ties." My soul ties began with my parents and others who connected with me in a sexual way. Even though some experiences I didn't want or accept, they became a bond to me mentally, emotionally and spiritually. They became like a stronghold for me. In everything, those strong ties influenced my choices throughout life. I didn't realize how much it controlled me until now.

The definition of a stronghold is this: a place that has been secured tightly in case of attack, or a place where a particular belief or ideology is firmly believed and staunchly defended.

In relating this to my studies, I came across a scripture from 2 Corinthians 10:4-5 (KJV). It reads, "For the weapons of our warfare are not carnal, but mighty through God to the pulling down of strongholds; Casting down imaginations, and every high thing that exalted itself against the knowledge of God, and bringing into captivity every thought to the obedience of Christ." I had been drawing myself to certain types of behaviors. They wouldn't let me go!

# Chapter 7

## Buried Alive

It's a new day! I made it through my childhood. I made it through some things in my young adult years. I even made it through some physical and mental abuse in my older years, and I am still going. I erased it all from my memory. I can't ever talk about it again. This is what I told myself daily. I had three healthy boys. We had a home for us to live in. We had food to eat. I had a car to drive. I had money in my pocket. "I AM GOOD!" It was time to bury the past. My boys and I deserved better. I am not going to allow my past to hurt them.

Yes, it's true that my father never told me I was a princess or how beautiful I was. He never showed me my value or how I was supposed to be treated by a man. Yes, my mother never showed me what to accept from a man; she never showed me not to accept anything but the best. I didn't see the respect from her. My self-esteem was so mutilated that I consented to any behavior. I wanted to make everything go away in my head and my heart, so I did. I buried it! I dedicated so much time trying to receive "love" from others. I was disappointed in myself. I was ashamed for allowing myself to be so loving and trusting. For years I lived in fear because of my past. My boys were my reasons to pull it together and keep pushing to survive.

Although I had my mother figures in my life, it wasn't the same. Who can take the place of the man and woman who birth me into this world? I couldn't call on "daddy" to give me some assurance that it was going to be ok after a heartbreak. My mother wasn't in the right mindset to give me any advice on any questions I had about finding the right love. I thought I buried my past and left it all behind, so now I am moving on.

All it took was one more argument for him to leave. It was too easy just to pack up and leave. What kept you from your family so easily? My ex-husband continued to test my trust. Maybe that was his agenda from the beginning. There was a special lady that took us under her wing in the last state where we once resided. We both confided in her and listened to her words of wisdom. It was hard to believe when she informed me of his plan to leave me once we relocated back to our home state. It was true. He was with another woman with three boys the same ages as ours. It was hurtful that everyone knew of his plan except me. I was naïve to his commitment to me.

I never thought I would have to take out a restraining

order against my ex-husband. He showed me a side of him that was familiar to my outer self. The anger was within him again, and I was the closest one for him to unload on. I will never forget his statement to me during an argument, "I have you on the south side, and I have her on the north side." He went to great lengths to intimidate me, and it worked. I was falling again into a realm of depression. I thought I buried you. Depression, why must you keep showing up in my life?

I had to make some decisions quickly for survival. I didn't have legal representation on how to protect myself after the divorce. I acted on my emotions and I just wanted out. I wished I never knew him to have put me through so much, but then again, I wouldn't be where I am at now. The feeling was real. It was over, or so I thought.

In my state of mind, I was still longing for love. I met another guy who seemed to get me, like really understand me. He was much younger than I and I enjoyed his company. He wined and dined me. That was what I needed; some special treatment, right? I was just getting back on my feet with a great job and my mindset together. What I didn't know was that he was just as insecure as I was in certain ways. It was like dealing with my child. We both had been dealing with our ex-spouses concerning our children. Red flags wavering, and I push them out the way. I didn't realize my heart was not quite healed from my ex. I tried telling my new friend what I was dealing with. He thought he could make it better by standing up to my ex-husband. Truth is, I really do believe I used him for a stand-in sex tool. It was the lust in me that said I needed him for just that. Truth is, he didn't stimulate me intellectually. I didn't feel financially secure or emotionally secure. I constantly had to tell him how to handle business for the household. He also questioned me about my whereabouts and became jealous if I failed to tell him anything. He had his own issues and insecurities, but again, I accepted it. This young man overall was an ok guy, so I married him—against my better judgment and his mother's judgment. We separated within less than a year and divorced two years later. My ex-husband and my new friend would have conversations when they met for the exchange for my younger son visits. My ex-husband spoke harsh about me and told him "She needs a strong man in her life."

The underlying feelings would sometimes surface, but I managed to cover it up with wishful thinking. I was good.

This couldn't be happening! One of my babies was sexually assaulted. This was a major flashback. My body and spirit went into a rage. I couldn't comprehend the magnitude of rage in me. I was ready to crush everybody who was involved. When my child told me the details of where and who, I was devastated. It was in his father's home. How did this happen? Where was the supervision? How could this happen under your care? What was worse was that his father said that I made it all up. What a horrible thing to make up. I knew the scars this would leave on him. My son's father didn't take this seriously. He didn't even show up for the counseling sessions with my son. "No More Miss Nice Girl;" it was war time! Forgiving was going out the door! I lost confidence in the court system after being humiliated by his father. To this day, his father has no clue of the impact on our son. This caused anger, anxiety, and cognitive fears.

Years later, my son was diagnosed with Attention Deficit Hyperactivity and Obsessive-Compulsive Disorder along with Anxiety. Now with counseling, he is dealing with memories of the different occurrences. This was something I couldn't just sit on. My child needed me. I would not allow this to keep him in bondage. What would my Nanny do? She would pray to God. I was hurting so bad that I couldn't pray. "We need you, God! Why is this happening to my child? Isn't this enough? When are you going to hear my cries?"

I needed guidance and understanding about this situation. I started attending counseling with my son. It reopened the wounds of my soul. It wasn't about me though. It was about my child getting what he needed. I put my guard up and closed the door again on the casket of my wounds. There was no time for me right then. My son had to heal from this, and I knew it was going to take some time. In the meantime, we were going to be ok, right?

Life went on, and it was moving on without me. My older boys were of the age to live on their own. There were unanswered questions with all of us. I didn't know how to talk to them about the concerns of our family. They seemed happy with their situations, but their behavior towards me showed otherwise. I wanted to bury it all in the unknown, hoping that it didn't come back, ever!

# Chapter 8

## The Bipolar Christian

My background did include some sort of church foundation. I saw my mother and father occasionally in church, but I never understood why the family fell apart. The saying, "A family that prays together, stays together," stayed in my head. We didn't pray together. Long as I could remember, I witnessed my Nanny in the church. She went through life, trusting God no matter what. I saw her belief. I just wanted that same belief she had.

Every place that I traveled, I had this urge to attend a church. I loved the choirs and a good word that I could relate to. Funny how God was trying to draw near to me the whole time. I believed it was the only way I could get through many things I encountered, but I wavered from time to time. I would go home and still deal with my inner self. I should have been happy. I should have been very proud. I had a beautiful home and car with just my name on it. A new career and a position doing what I loved to do. I was mending some relationships back together, and life was good. Why was I still unhappy inside? What was missing?

I was trying to stay focused on raising my younger son and granddaughter. She's the daughter I never had. I was nervous about taking on this task, but grateful that I did. She's been a blessing in disguise. I could see myself in her. This generational curse will stop with me. I am determined to protect her from enduring anything that I went through. God, you have given me the opportunity to get this right again. What's next?

Church is supposed to be a safe place. It's a place to meet God as you are and get educated on God's word and fellowship among believers. I would see the miracles happening and see people delivered in many churches. I would hear of their testimonies and be in awe. I wanted this so bad for my situation long ago. I needed it now. Out of formality, I would go to church searching for answers. Tears would stream down my face when a song or sermon touched me in a special way. I believed God was trying to reach me, but I was holding on to some pain in my heart. On the outside, the church people would see me and compliment me on my hair and makeup. "Girl, you're always on point…. You're so beautiful and strong…. You're doing such a great job with those kids…. God's going to bless you for all that you do." If they could see all this in me, why was it that I couldn't see it for myself? What they didn't know was that pain and heartache were hidden behind the mask of makeup. They had no idea of the panic attacks I would have every so often. My doctor would prescribe stimulants to help me, but I would refuse to take them. I was terrified of ending up like my mother. I could do this on my own.

Since I wasn't really a club girl and not so aggressive with approaching men, I was tempted from attention from men who I thought was out my league. I knew my weakness but ignored my shortcomings as I continued looking for love in the wrong places. What could go wrong in church? If they were in the church, maybe that means they have some sort of religious background, right? My outer-self needed some comfort, and my inner-self needed some deliverance. It was a battle that I didn't know how to conquer, so I found myself caught up with someone again. He didn't know he was a tool for my outer self. Even though my outer-self craved intimacy, my inner-self hated it. It happened several times: my outer-self was temporarily satisfied, but my inner-self was left ashamed. How could I worship now in the church? Well, they say you are forgiven, so I repented. I was good, right?

I thought I had my outer self under control. I was doing well with everything. I was naïve to think someone would be that brave and slick to assault women in the church. This church member was obviously comfortable making inappropriate comments and acts to other ladies in the church. He even offered rides to certain ones who didn't have a car. He would do little odd jobs and favors for all the ladies. It's no wonder why the wife started accusing him of cheating with a certain woman in the church. This church member demon would give money here and there to the children of the women he showed interest to. I never thought too much about it when he offered to help with repairs to my car. I could use a discount, being that I was a single mom. I didn't think too much of it when he offered to bring some equipment to my home that I borrowed from the church. I looked at him as a father figure. After bringing in the equipment, he left money on the table. He said it was a "housewarming gift." He began talking about intimate things about his wife. He said she had accused him of cheating with me as well. He drew close to me and started kissing me fiercely while attempting to undo my clothes all the same time. I yelled at him, "You dirty bastard!" Something inside me started to hit and kick. I threatened him and pushed him to get out. It was not even 20 minutes later that I received a text message of apology. It stated, "My wife was always jealous of you. You got it going on with your house and car. Keep it between us. I just got beside myself." I couldn't believe this has just happened. Who can I call? Who can I trust!

You wouldn't believe who I called. My ex-husband! I told him what happen. I was distraught. What could he do? Just for the moment, I wanted to trust he could help me.

After confiding in someone else, I got up enough nerve to take it to the church. I was back in court again as that little 15-year-old with high school boys. I was questioned of my intent in having him at my house. I was questioned about the monies received. I was even questioned about the conversations. He had a title in the church, and I didn't. He was looked upon as a person that had favor. I was looked upon as the one in the wrong.

This set me back and took me to a place where I didn't trust people in the church the same way again. They didn't treat me any differently than people outside the church. I couldn't attend that church anymore. To see this person at the place that was supposed to be my safe haven was humiliating. I don't think the pastors understood my reasons. At the time, it didn't matter to me what they thought of me. They only knew what I wanted them to know about me. So many had opinions about why I left the church. I was told not to run away from the church and not to isolate myself. They had no idea how this just added to my issues about men. I was on the road to redemption, but my faith was fading again. Wrong is wrong in my eyes. I later learned of others speaking out on similar assaults from the same guy.

My inner self knew I needed help to live.

2 Corinthians 4:17-18 (NLT):

For our present troubles are small and won't last very long. Yet they produce for us a glory that vastly outweighs them and will last forever! We don't look at the troubles we can see now; rather, we fix our gaze on things that cannot be seen. For the things we see now will soon be gone, but the things we cannot see will last forever.

# Chapter 9

# Internal War

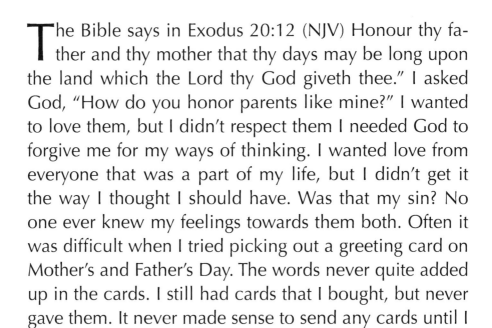

The Bible says in Exodus 20:12 (NJV) Honour thy father and thy mother that thy days may be long upon the land which the Lord thy God giveth thee." I asked God, "How do you honor parents like mine?" I wanted to love them, but I didn't respect them I needed God to forgive me for my ways of thinking. I wanted love from everyone that was a part of my life, but I didn't get it the way I thought I should have. Was that my sin? No one ever knew my feelings towards them both. Often it was difficult when I tried picking out a greeting card on Mother's and Father's Day. The words never quite added up in the cards. I still had cards that I bought, but never gave them. It never made sense to send any cards until I understood why I felt a certain way about them.

My Nanny was so precious to me. I often thought to myself, "What if she was still alive? Would I have made so many unhealthy choices back then?" She was the only one that I respected enough to halfway listen to. She always told me, "Don't take any wooden nickels from anyone," meaning that I should be careful to not fall for anything from anyone that only appears to be real. Yet I failed so many times with that saying. What good did it do to forgive people and still be a pushover? I pushed certain ones away from me; they could no longer hurt me if I was no longer around.

I was having mental breakdowns throughout my life but didn't realize it. I was just living my life as if I had no past. I was so busy working and being a mommy that I didn't see my own turmoil. How did I make it this far without being in a mental facility because of my emotions? I was super mom, super wife, maid, cook, secretary, mechanic, yard worker, advocate for the school, churchgoer, mediator and driver, just to name a few. I needed self-care myself, but there wasn't time for that. Yes, I was prescribed stimulants, but I refused to take them because the fear of getting hooked on meds was devastating. There was no way I was going to end up like my mother.

It was obvious to me that I had a strong alternate ego. Angie is what I'll call her. She would never let me down. I was co-dependent on her. I could depend on her to stick with me through thick and thin. She would fight you with her words in a sarcastic way. She put the gate up with hard iron chains and protected me when I couldn't fight anymore. She knew I wanted to have peace and happiness, but she also knew my weakness. When I found myself in situations, she pushed me to shake it off and get my act together. See, the only thing about Angie is she didn't like for me to hurt. She didn't forgive some people or even forgive me for many choices I made.

I, on the other hand, was heartbroken from past relationships. I felt the depression. I went through the anxiety of remembering certain trauma. I had multiple nightmares. I wrestled with taunting spirits every night. I had regrets of not leaving toxic relationships. I was too nice to others who took advantage of me—mostly males. That's another thing. I never was close to any females other than my grandmother. Maybe if I had some true girlfriends or a real sister to encourage me back then, I would have gotten through some hard times I was dealing with. Who knows? I had enough of the past repeating itself in my life; I was determined to live.

I had an "I am an independent lady who doesn't need a man attitude," but behind closed doors, I still needed what I was exposed to in the past. It's because of this soul tie within me that I just kept getting myself in similar situations with just a friend.

I was addicted to having a man in my life, even if it killed me. See, the outside of me still craved love and affection. I deserved to be loved too. What's taking so long for my Boaz? I was actually proud of myself for being on what I thought was the road to recovery.

My scenarios seem to just keep repeating itself. The craving to be held by someone who loved me with all my insecurities was still with me. I always saw the good in someone if they showed me a different side of what I was used to. With most of my adult male relationships, my vulnerability attracted the sense of manipulation. I showed that my guard was willing to open the gate with just a kind word or gesture from them. I was willing to give my all too fast. Although, the heart was broken, scarred, and tainted, it still was soft for love. My spirit showed a motherly love to take care of home.

Basically, I was ready for my predators to pounce on me at any given time.

John 10:10 (KJV)

The thief cometh not, but for to steal and to kill and to destroy I am come that they might have life, and that they might have it more abundantly.

My assignment needed to be shut down. My assigned spirit came to destroy what was ordained for my purpose to come forth. It was always attracted to me because I showed a sense of desperation. I was always attracted to it because of the sense of strength and protection. It looked very charming, it felt good, and always smelled so appealing. It came with kind words, dinners, special gifts, and getaways. I was hooked if it showed love to my kids. It wasn't hard for me to fall in love because it was something I needed. It wasn't hard for me to commit. I went off my impulse of wishfully thinking that this was for me. If it came to me, I would think it's finally happening. The only thing about these relationships, it didn't know all of who I was. It had no idea of my trauma until it was exposed with familiarity.

Beyond my beliefs, I made moves to start relationships with different religious backgrounds. I grew emotionally involved with it. I wanted it no matter what. I trusted it. I respected it. I changed for it. I loved it more than myself. I tried being someone else in order to be accepted by it. I was committed and submissive but didn't receive it in return. See, my demons never left me; they were sleeping and waiting for the right time to come out.

See, I had what they called "A woman's intuition" that would often tug at my heart and mind, that something was not always right. It was recognizable. The lack of boundaries with other women and the disrespect were triggers for my open door of betrayal. Despite the warnings and deception in my face, I still was in denial with these relationships. It was supposed to make me crazy and make me appear as a paranoid person. It was doing a great job on my mental state. Broken men were attracted to my brokenness. In other words, I attracted the same spirit every time because I didn't know my worth.

I sought counseling and wondered why I was going through this similar scenario time after time. What did I do wrong? I gave my heart too soon. I slowly began to spiral in my life. My past pain and hurts were coming to the forefront. My alternate ego came forth, my protector. She reacted in a way that was out of character. I was angry with myself for allowing someone to take me there. I would scream with fear and curse in rebuttal to the insults. I was angry with the person for not being who I wanted them to be for me. They would fail to protect my heart, just like my father failed. They knew of my hurtful experiences and trauma that happened in my life and used it against me. How could they help me if they had their own issues and insecurities? It was the same scene, just with different characters.

We were all major proof that "hurt people, hurt people." Every ounce of my body became a mental and emotional punching bag to every reminder of my past. I had fallen into a state of depression so many times. This time, I was able to dictate and point out the root cause of everything, but then I started to become a person that I didn't like to see in the mirror. I didn't like myself anymore. My appearance was so ugly to me that I considered enhancement surgery. The person in the mirror spoke to me every time I saw her. She was enraged with everyone who hurt her all over again. In her head, no one loved her. She wasn't good enough to be a mother. She wasn't enough for any man to love her. She wasn't educated enough to have a career that brought her prestige. She couldn't articulate enough to get the respect that she demanded. Her inner enemy inside her head told her to give it all up. "Your children are better off without you. They don't respect you, either. They can do better with their other parents. Your own parents don't love you. Look at what they did to you. You're done!" I felt hopeless and worthless.

After having a private pity party, I started to go back to God and ask for the "eleventh-hour" help. I cried out, "God, help me with every situation!" God showed me my actions that were not in agreement with his written word in the Bible. The book of Ephesians in the Holy Bible was my study guide for one month. I felt like I was whipped by each chapter as I read with gratitude.

All this time, I was going to church and didn't know the true word. I never asked God for direction in making a choice to marry or be in an intimate relationship. It seemed the closer I got to God, the worse all my relationships became. I finally let go of trying to please others in a way I thought would get them to love me. I had to let God do his miraculous work in me. I had a sick soul. My unwanted and wanted soul-ties to individuals caused a warring of my own connection to God.

Remember what a soul-tie refers to—a spiritual and emotional connection from one person to another. I was exposed to relationships that didn't agree with my relationship with God. I wanted what I desired, but I was miserable trying to keep it. Although I knew about premarital sex before marriage, I never knew of the true consequences. You will take on spiritual soul-ties from that person and their partners as well. Imagine yourself and your ex-sex partners with your spouse and all their ex-sex partners in the same bed. "Humm," this makes you think about all those personalities and spirits you've been dealing with or that have been causing you to act and behave in a certain way. I started praying in a fervent prayer and speaking to my inner self as well as my outer flesh. I had to allow my heart to break into many pieces so that my soul could be corrected. It was war time with God on my side! I had to allow God to make me whole again before I could love and receive love.

Ephesians 6:12 (The Living Bible):

For we are not fighting against people made of flesh and blood, but against persons without bodies—the evil rulers of the unseen world, those mighty satanic beings and great evil princes of darkness who rule this world; and against huge numbers of wicked spirits in the spirit world.

# Chapter 10

## Purposely Chosen

The cost of my innocence, my heart, my mindset, my self-esteem, my pain, my rejection, my depression, my anxiety, my will, and my desire to receive love was the cost of the oil in my alabaster box. For the precious oil to be restored, the vessel had to be broken. It was costly in my eyes, but nothing can compare to the cost of what Jesus paid for my life. I never knew why I had to endure such trauma and abuse in my life until now. I never knew the purpose. God knew what I could endure better than I knew for myself. I had to face these hurts so that I could reach those who have also encountered similar situations. They need to know there's hope, and that they will survive. When you don't give up on yourself, you win. I truly believe there's a purpose in all things. I had to learn my true value. I had to accept that I was given this task for a reason. God was preparing me for such a time as this.

It has been a process to heal in certain areas of my life. It was necessary for the events to occur in my early childhood years up to my adult life. Every person was orchestrated to be part of the plan, even down to my mother, who birthed me into this world when she could have aborted me, and my father, whose sperm was used to create me. For every boy, man, or person who caused any hurt, pain, disappointment, or stress in my life, I forgive you. You were assigned to my purpose. You might have meant it for evil, but God meant for good. It was painful, but God brought me through it to be who I am today. I am stronger in so many ways. Experience was my best teacher. By the Grace of God, I am living with no regrets for all that I had to endure. I am grateful for discernment. I know my worth and won't stand for nonsense. Yes, it's been a challenge, but I take one day at a time, getting stronger every day. Each day I must start with prayer to remove any lingering negative thoughts that come my way, guarding my mind against destruction daily and guarding my heart.

My healing came with facing my past and present. I had to deal with the root of the matter. It may go away temporarily, but it's still there and will pop its head up when you least expect it. I had to learn to forgive myself truly and not allow my past mistakes to overtake me. I have an opportunity to use my pain for a purpose now. I have a Heavenly Father who loves me unconditionally. Even though I forgave, I choose to deal with certain people from a distance. Sometimes people try to test who you say you are and provoke you. Everyone must deal with their own demons at some point, unless they are comfortable with their status.

Although I wondered where God was during every scene of my life, he was right there, covering me the whole time. He didn't allow me to go forth with any suicide attempts. He allowed me to go to sleep and rest when I needed it. He allowed me to get up each day and attend to my children. They were never neglected or deprived of my love and nurturing.

No one knows the pain of physical, emotional, mental, or sexual abuse unless you have gone through it. It makes me sick to my stomach to hear someone say "get over it" when they do not understand the battles that person must fight daily. Every day is a fight. Now, I understand why my mother treated me the way she did. Her abuse led to her mental illness for years. My heart feels compassion and empathy for her instead of hatred. It bothers me to see her in her condition. God is still healing our relationship. My father has not reached out to me since I wrote him a letter confronting him of my memories. It's truly ok. I did my part.

I am determined to stop the generational curses within my family and other families by speaking out. I won't be ashamed of the process. No one should feel reluctant to share their story if it's going to help someone else. My voice will be heard, and I will make a difference everywhere I go. This assignment will not return void.

The reward will be great, and I won't give up on my sons. I won't give up on my grandchildren. Our emotions are restored after any type of abuse! We are conquering all things that are meant to destroy us! We are all Purposely Chosen!

St. John 8:32 (The Living Bible):

And you will know the truth, and the truth will set you free.

# Conclusion

Finally, I had to realize this journey caused me some pain and longsuffering in my life. It wasn't easy to accept. I often asked, "How could God allow so much to happen in a person's life if he really loves them?" Then I was answered, "How can I use you if you haven't been through it yourself?"

We all have a purpose to help nurture someone, but we are only attracted to whom we can relate to. I learned many lessons, and I am sure I will have more to learn as long as I live. We can't give up on ourselves. I know it is easily said than done, but once you realize the root of it all, you must let go of shame. You will then become a new person. You must recognize it, name it, and then release it. Any abuse is not your fault. When you keep shame a secret, it will gain power over you. You are enough to have what you want in life, with all your jacked-up mess. It's never too late to turn it around.

God has given me a vision to help others by starting a non-profit support group, Restoration After Children's Emotions (R.A.C.E.). This group will mentor young girls and women who have endured and struggled with unimaginable difficulties. R.A.C.E will be a safe place to share with someone that truly understands you. We will offer resources and counseling referrals for those who have had unwanted or abusive experiences that may have affected their mental and emotional health.

R.A.C.E will give people an opportunity to pursue their dreams with support, despite the challenges they may have faced in their lives. You can live your life again with God and the right support.

Trusting the plan for my life has influenced the shape of my character. No more pain, no more shame, no more feeling guilty about it. No more living in dysfunction. I will no longer allow anyone to make a mockery of my will to heal. Exposing the demons that haunted me for years is dismissed from my peripheral and rearview vision now. I had to wake up and decide to face my fears, or I was going to die a slow death of heartbreak. My healing process has changed my habits of accepting anything that will come my way, with courage. God created me for this task. I was called because I was flawed. I thought I had to change my looks to have someone. All I had to do was change my mindset. I am Amazing! I don't have to beg, force or chase anyone or anything. Instead, I will pray, have faith, and put into action what God has for me. Therefore, my destiny won't be aborted. I will stay focused and live on purpose to help my sisters and brothers who need restoration in their lives.

You and I have a choice to be bitter or angry with our past. We can make the decision to turn our hurts around and share with others about our healing and forgiving in our journey. That's how we heal and grow: by helping others get on the road to recovery. When you believe God, you position yourself for a miracle. When you speak and believe His words, you open the door to His Power in your life. Protect your mind and heart with the words of wisdom. Your trials came to make you strong. It's ok to be you; everyone else is taken. You deserve to be loved and happy, Queens and Kings. You are worth it. You're only a decision away from a totally different life. Seek God's face and let him direct you. Even if you mess up and fall back, it's ok. He will not condemn you and will help you start all over again. God uses broken people like you and me to rescue other broken people. You never know who is watching your journey, so get up and go! Say affirmations to yourself every day. Simple words can make a difference in your life. Say, "I AM STRONG! I AM POWERFUL! I AM WORTHY! I AM CONFIDENT! I AM ENOUGH! I HAVE WHAT IT TAKES TO MAKE IT!" Fall in love with yourself before chasing the heart of someone else.

Forgive yourself. Heal completely. Accept yourself. Value yourself. Empower yourself. Love yourself. God has a plan for true love to find you. God will give you what you need. Imagine that, He was there the whole time with me, like "footprints in the sand." What a friend He has been. He will be your mother and your father.

He will be closer than any other. He will see you through to the end! You have the Power to change your life!

Psalm 139:13-16 (MSG):

*Oh yes, you shaped me first inside, then out;*

*you formed me in my mother's womb.*

*I thank you, High God—you're breathtaking!*

*Body and soul, I am marvelously made!*

*I worship in adoration—what a creation!*

*You know me inside and out,*

*You know every bone in my body;*

*You know exactly how I was made, bit by bit, how I was sculpted from nothing into something.*

*Like an open book, you watched me grow from conception to birth;*

*all the stages of my life were spread out before you,*

*The days of my life all prepared before I'd even lived one day.*

# "The Fishbowl"
## By Young Angelee

*I see them looking at me.*

*What do they really see?*

*Do they see my scars?*

*Or is it true, I am from Mars?*

*Is it possible to live free?*

*No, the fishbowl is where I am me.*

*Wait, someone is coming for me.*

*Lift me up, tell me I can be free.*

*It's not so bad out here after all.*

*It was all in my head, that I didn't have a ball!*

# "A Special Thank You"
## By Amazing Angelee

*Thanks to those who hated me,*

*You made me stronger.*

*Thanks to those that loved me,*

*You made my heart go fonder.*

*Thanks to those who cared,*

*You made me feel important.*

*Thanks to those who entered my life,*

*You made me who I am today.*

*Thanks to those who left,*

*You showed me that nothing last forever.*

*Thanks to those who stayed,*

*You showed me true friendship.*

*Thanks to those who listened,*

*You made me feel like I was worth it.*

# "God's Response to My Prayers"

*"You held on during the toughest of times.*

*I gave you strength to endure that at times, you did not even know it was me.*

*When things changed for you, many left you and wrote you off.*

*But not only did you endure the storm…you grew in the storm.*

*Yes, you are different…I did not create you to fit in.*

*I created you to stand out.*

*Now I am about to Bless your faithfulness.*

*I am about to take you to levels you never even thought were possible!"*

*Receive it in My Name,*

*In Jesus Christ Name*


-   Author Unknown

# "If the Tables Were Turned"
## By Amazing Angelee

*If the tables were turned*

*As your mommy, I would have held you in my loving arms and told you, "I Love You"*

*Instead, I left you with a familiar enemy you knew*

*If the tables were turned*

*As your father, I would have protected you from all the evil games*

*Instead, I touched you in places that left you ashamed*

*If the tables were turned*

*As your lover, I would have called you beautiful and sweetheart*

*But without any regrets, I called you less and broke your heart*

*If the tables were turned*

*As your Creator, I would have allowed you to see baby #3*

*But just trust that it was best for her to rest with me*

*And now that the tables have turned*

*I've found a love that is healing things that I can't even see*

*He promised me he'd love me unconditionally*

*With all my flaws, mess ups and falls*

*He still answers when I call*

*My life has become a living witness*

*Today I can now live in forgiveness*

*Anxiety, Depression, Guilt, & Shame*

*Settling for less, I no longer claim*

*Today and tomorrow, I have a choice*

*To take a stand and project my voice*

*God has blessed me to be free*

*Amazing Grace brought forth Amazing Angelee*

# I AM

Every day remind yourself of who you are. Take the time to write your own affirmations and recite daily. The first one is on me. You are Purposely Chosen!

1. _____

2. _____

3. _____

4. _____

5. _____

6. _____

7. _____

8. _____

9. _____

10. _____

# Notes:

# Notes:

# Notes:

# References:

1. Laura Davis, *The Courage to Heal Workbook For Women and Men Survivors of Sexual Abuse*

2. R.C. Blakes, Jr., *Soul Ties, Breaking the Ties That Bind*

3.Randy Peterson, *Why Me God? Trusting God in Times of Trouble*

4. Joyce Meyer , *The Root of Rejection*

5.The Living Bible

6. King James Version

7. The Message Bible

8. New Living Translation

Made in the USA
Columbia, SC
04 December 2019